MW01194538

TO:

....

Through wisdom your days
will be many, and years
will be added to your life.

PROVERBS 9:11

FROM:

....

DEVOTIONS FOR
GRANDMAS

ZONDERVAN®

ZONDERVAN

Devotions for Grandmas

Published in Grand Rapids, Michigan, by Zondervan. Zondervan is a registered trademark of The Zondervan Corporation, L.L.C., a wholly owned subsidiary of HarperCollins Christian Publishing, Inc.

Requests for information should be addressed to customercare@harpercollins.com.

ISBN 978-0-310-46730-4 (HC)
ISBN 978-0-310-46732-8 (eBook)

Art direction: Gabriella Wikidal
Interior design: Kristy Edwards

Printed in Malaysia

25 26 27 28 29 OFF 10 9 8 7 6 5 4 3 2 1

CONTENTS

Even when I am old and gray,

do not forsake me, my God,

till I declare your power

to the next generation,

your mighty acts to all who are to come.

PSALM 71:18

1

WISDOM FOUND

I like the question once asked by Satchel Paige, that venerable alumnus of baseball: "How old would you be if you didn't know how old you were?" An honest answer to that question depends on an honest admission of one's attitude. It has nothing to do with one's age.

The longer I live, the more I become convinced that our major battle in life is not with age but with maturity. There is no choice involved in growing older. God's goal is that we move toward maturity, all our past failures and faults and hang-ups notwithstanding.

Let me leave you three bones to chew on:

1. *Look within and release.* What is stunting your growth? Let it go.
2. *Look around and respond.* Is there some need you can help meet? Risk responding.
3. *Look up and rejoice.* You are the recipient of His riches! And the more involved you remain, the less concern you will have for how old you are.

By the way, how old would you be if you didn't know how old you were?

—Charles R. Swindoll

GOD'S WORDS FOR YOU, GRANDMA

"Even to your old age and gray hairs I am he, I am he who will sustain you. I have made you and I will carry you; I will sustain you and I will rescue you."

ISAIAH 46:4

They will still bear fruit in old age, they will stay fresh and green, proclaiming, "The LORD is upright; he is my Rock, and there is no wickedness in him."

PSALM 92:14-15

Gray hair is a crown of splendor; it is attained in the way of righteousness.

PROVERBS 16:31

The glory of young men is their strength, gray hair the splendor of the old.

PROVERBS 20:29

May the favor of the Lord our God rest on us; establish the work of our hands for us—yes, establish the work of our hands.

PSALM 90:17

He asked you for life, and you gave it to him—length of days, for ever and ever.

PSALM 21:4

Teach us to number our days, that we may gain a heart of wisdom.

PSALM 90:12

The fear of the Lord adds length to life.

PROVERBS 10:27

"With long life I will satisfy him and show him my salvation."

PSALM 91:16

"Is not wisdom found among the aged? Does not long life bring understanding?"

JOB 12:12

My goal is that they may be encouraged in heart and united in love, so that they may have the full riches of complete understanding, in order that they may know the mystery of God, namely, Christ, in whom are hidden all the treasures of wisdom and knowledge.

COLOSSIANS 2:2–3

2

THE LIVING WORD OF GOD

You're unleashing unkind words at your husband when suddenly into your mind comes a phrase: "Do not let any unwholesome talk come out of your mouths" (Ephesians 4:29). Where did this come from?

You're flipping through a home-decorating magazine when another phrase comes into your thoughts: "I have learned to be content whatever the circumstances" (Philippians 4:11). Amazing!

In 2 Timothy 3:16, Paul wrote, "All Scripture is God-breathed and is useful for teaching, rebuking, correcting and training in righteousness." What we read in the Bible are God's words, spoken through human instruments, passed down orally and then finally written. God's words continue to speak even today to all who read and listen.

In 2 Timothy 3:16, Paul stressed four functions of the living Word. Teaching—it imparts to us information about truth and God. Rebuking—it tells us when we are wrong. Correcting—it redirects us when we stray. Training—it prepares us for each next step of becoming like Him.

The Bible is God's actual living Word. He speaks when we read it. And He speaks again in our day-to-day experience when He helps us recall what He says.

—Elisa Morgan

GOD'S WORDS FOR YOU, GRANDMA

Everything that was written in the past was written to teach us, so that through the endurance taught in the Scriptures and the encouragement they provide we might have hope.

ROMANS 15:4

The word of God is alive and active. Sharper than any double-edged sword, it penetrates even to dividing soul and spirit, joints and marrow; it judges the thoughts and attitudes of the heart.

HEBREWS 4:12

Like newborn babies, crave pure spiritual milk, so that by it you may grow up in your salvation.

1 PETER 2:2

Oh, how I love your law! I meditate on it all day long.

PSALM 119:97

"Let us discern for ourselves what is right; let us learn together what is good."

JOB 34:4

Grow in the grace and knowledge of our Lord and Savior Jesus Christ. To him be glory both now and forever! Amen.

2 PETER 3:18

Your statutes are my heritage forever; they are the joy of my heart.

PSALM 119:111

This is my prayer: that your love may abound more and more in knowledge and depth of insight, so that you may be able to discern what is best and may be pure and blameless for the day of Christ.

PHILIPPIANS 1:9–10

Keep this Book of the Law always on your lips; meditate on it day and night, so that you may be careful to do everything written in it. Then you will be prosperous and successful.

JOSHUA 1:8

The unfolding of your words gives light; it gives understanding to the simple.

PSALM 119:130

Hold on to what is good. . . . May God himself, the God of peace, sanctify you through and through. May your whole spirit, soul and body be kept blameless at the coming of our Lord Jesus Christ.

1 THESSALONIANS 5:21, 23

3

BONDS OF A PLEDGE

Sins of all kinds are all around us—and inside us. How can we break free from them and be distinctive people in Christ?

Daniel disregarded the popular beliefs of his day and lived instead by God's standards. The "Daniel woman" doesn't walk out on her family. She doesn't hang up on her daughter. She doesn't ignore her neighbor's needs. She doesn't insist on playing the game of life by her own rules but rather chooses to play consistently, obediently, sometimes even painfully, by God's design. She stays committed to those around her. She recognizes and respects the bonds of a pledge, whether to a husband, a child, or her God.

In our day, avoiding consequences and ignoring promises are all too common, but the woman who stands by her commitment and fights for healthy relationships is a "Daniel woman": a distinctive person in Christ.

—Elisa Morgan

GOD'S WORDS FOR YOU, GRANDMA

Let us not become weary in doing good, for at the proper time we will reap a harvest if we do not give up.

GALATIANS 6:9

"Be strong and do not give up, for your work will be rewarded."

2 CHRONICLES 15:7

"May your hearts be fully committed to the LORD our God, to live by his decrees and obey his commands."

1 KINGS 8:61

Serve wholeheartedly, as if you were serving the Lord, not people, because you know that the Lord will reward each one for whatever good they do.

EPHESIANS 6:7–8

Place me like a seal over your heart, like a seal on your arm; for love is as strong as death.

SONG OF SONGS 8:6

"Blessed is the one who trusts in the LORD, whose confidence is in him."

JEREMIAH 17:7

Anyone who runs ahead and does not continue in the teaching of Christ does not have God; whoever continues in the teaching has both the Father and the Son.

2 JOHN V. 9

Never be lacking in zeal, but keep your spiritual fervor, serving the Lord.

ROMANS 12:11

"Whoever acknowledges me before others, I will also acknowledge before my Father in heaven."

MATTHEW 10:32

"I am coming soon. Hold on to what you have, so that no one will take your crown."

REVELATION 3:11

I press on toward the goal to win the prize for which God has called me heavenward in Christ Jesus.

PHILIPPIANS 3:14

The LORD is my rock, my fortress and my deliverer; my God is my rock, in whom I take refuge, my shield and the horn of my salvation, my stronghold.

PSALM 18:2

May these words of my mouth
and this meditation of my heart
be pleasing in your sight LORD
my Rock and my Redeemer.

PSALM 19:14

4

DAILY CONVERSATIONS

Someone coined a phrase to describe how the early church in Jerusalem went about spreading the Gospel. It was called "gossiping the Gospel"—integrating the Gospel into everyday conversation. There were no tracts, books, or Bibles to hand out. Rather, witnessing was a matter of word of mouth wherever people went.

That idea is found in Deuteronomy 6:4–9, where Moses instructed parents on how to pass on the requirements of the covenant, the details of God's law, to their children. He said to talk to the children in the house and in the street, when you're going to bed and when you rise up—and everywhere in between. It was a common Hebrew way of expressing the idea of totality—the two ends of the spectrum included everything in between. But it doesn't mean simply to teach children the contents of the covenant. It meant to illustrate how the covenant applied to daily life—in the home, in the street, in the market, and "everywhere in between."

How often in a day do you grasp the opportunity to integrate God's truth into your daily conversations—especially with those who are not believers?

—Dr. David Jeremiah

GOD'S WORDS FOR YOU, GRANDMA

[Paul] traveled through that area, speaking many words of encouragement to the people.

ACTS 20:2

Be wise in the way you act toward outsiders; make the most of every opportunity.

COLOSSIANS 4:5

Do not let any unwholesome talk come out of your mouths, but only what is helpful for building others up according to their needs, that it may benefit those who listen.

EPHESIANS 4:29

My mouth will speak words of wisdom.

PSALM 49:3

The prudent hold their tongues.

PROVERBS 10:19

Put off falsehood and speak truthfully to your neighbor.

EPHESIANS 4:25

Let your conversation be always full of grace, seasoned with salt, so that you may know how to answer everyone.

COLOSSIANS 4:6

Be filled with the Spirit, speaking to one another with psalms, hymns, and songs from the Spirit.

EPHESIANS 5:18–19

The words of the mouth are deep waters, but the fountain of wisdom is a rushing stream.

PROVERBS 18:4

"A good man brings good things out of the good stored up in his heart. . . . For the mouth speaks what the heart is full of."

LUKE 6:45

You are my hiding place; you will protect me from trouble and surround me with songs of deliverance.

PSALM 32:7

The name of the LORD is a fortified tower; the righteous run to it and are safe.

PROVERBS 18:10

May these words of my mouth

and this meditation of my heart

be pleasing in your sight,

5

EVERYWHERE IN BETWEEN

Someone coined a phrase to describe how the early church in Jerusalem went about spreading the gospel. It was called "gossiping the gospel"—integrating the gospel into everyday conversation. There were no tracts, books, or Bibles to hand out. Rather, witnessing was a matter of word of mouth wherever people went.

That idea is found in Deuteronomy 6:4–9 where Moses instructed parents on how to pass on the requirements of the covenant, the details of God's law, to their children. He said to talk to the children in the house and in the street, when you're going to bed and when you rise up—and everywhere in between. It was a common Hebrew way of expressing the idea of totality—the two ends of the spectrum included everything in between. But it doesn't mean simply to teach children the contents of the covenant. It meant to illustrate how the covenant applied to daily life—in the home, in the street, in the market, and "everywhere in between."

How often in a day do you grasp the opportunity to integrate God's truth into your daily conversations—especially with those who are not believers?

—Dr. David Jeremiah

GOD'S WORDS FOR YOU, GRANDMA

[Paul] traveled through that area, speaking many words of encouragement to the people.

ACTS 20:2

Be wise in the way you act toward outsiders; make the most of every opportunity.

COLOSSIANS 4:5

Do not let any unwholesome talk come out of your mouths, but only what is helpful for building others up according to their needs, that it may benefit those who listen.

EPHESIANS 4:29

My mouth will speak words of wisdom.

PSALM 49:3

The prudent hold their tongues.

PROVERBS 10:19

Speaking the truth in love, we will grow to become in every respect the mature body of him who is the head, that is, Christ.

EPHESIANS 4:15

Put off falsehood and speak truthfully to your neighbor.

EPHESIANS 4:25

Let your conversation be always full of grace, seasoned with salt, so that you may know how to answer everyone.

COLOSSIANS 4:6

The lips of the righteous nourish many. . . .
From the mouth of the righteous comes the fruit of wisdom.

PROVERBS 10:21, 31

The mouths of the righteous utter wisdom,
and their tongues speak what is just.

PSALM 37:30

Be filled with the Spirit, speaking to one another with psalms, hymns, and songs from the Spirit.

EPHESIANS 5:18–19

The words of the mouth are deep waters,
but the fountain of wisdom is a rushing stream.

PROVERBS 18:4

"A good man brings good things out of the good stored up in his heart. . . . For the mouth speaks what the heart is full of."

LUKE 6:45

Have compassion on your servants.

Satisfy us in the morning

with your unfailing love,

that we may sing for joy

and be glad all our days.

PSALM 90:13–14

6

COMPASSIONATE LOVE

The truly loving person hands out compassion in free and generous doses. God likens true compassion to a mother's empathy for her child. This could also be applied to a grandmother. Who will rise in the middle of the night to hold a grandchild with a fever? Who will run back to the store to pick up one more item for a grandchild's school project? Who will reinforce discipline by firmly adhering to an unpopular restriction?

A grandmother whose heart is filled with compassion.

God shows His compassion to us in that He sent Christ to die for us while we were still sinners (Romans 5:8). God nurses our wounds even though He isn't the one who caused them. When our bodies drag and our spirits sag, it takes a heart committed to God and the infiltrating power of His Holy Spirit to be compassionate. It takes God—with the heart of a grandmother—to bring compassion to those who need it.

Lean into the compassionate love of God. Sigh. Rest.

Then offer what you've been given—freely, lavishly—to those around you.

—Elisa Morgan

GOD'S WORDS FOR YOU, GRANDMA

"The Lord your God is gracious and compassionate. He will not turn his face from you if you return to him."

2 CHRONICLES 30:9

The Lord is good to all; he has compassion on all he has made.

PSALM 145:9

Praise the Lord, my soul, . . . who redeems your life from the pit and crowns you with love and compassion, who satisfies your desires with good things so that your youth is renewed like the eagle's.

PSALM 103:2, 4–5

The Lord longs to be gracious to you; therefore he will rise up to show you compassion.

ISAIAH 30:18

Praise be to the God and Father of our Lord Jesus Christ, the Father of compassion. . . . Our comfort abounds through Christ.

2 CORINTHIANS 1:3, 5

"He who has compassion on them will guide them and lead them beside springs of water. . . .

For the Lord comforts his people and will have compassion on his afflicted ones."

ISAIAH 49:10, 13

"On the day when I act," says the Lord Almighty, "they will be my treasured possession. I will spare them, just as a father has compassion and spares his son who serves him."

MALACHI 3:17

Jesus had compassion on them and touched their eyes. Immediately they received their sight and followed him.

MATTHEW 20:34

Return to the Lord your God,
 for he is gracious and compassionate,
 slow to anger and abounding in love,
 and he relents from sending calamity.

JOEL 2:13

"You will not have to fight this battle. Take up your positions; stand firm and see the deliverance the Lord will give you. . . . Do not be afraid; do not be discouraged."

2 CHRONICLES 20:17

I remain confident of this:

I will see the goodness of the LORD

in the land of the living.

PSALM 27:13

7

ETERNAL INHERITANCE

First John is in your Bible for one main reason: to provide confidence to believers who are struggling with doubt. John wrote to encourage followers of Jesus and to remind them eternal life awaits them.

Here in this life, although we have not yet received our eternal inheritance, we have access to all of the resources of God through prayer. God promises "that if we ask anything according to His will, He hears us" (1 John 5:14 NKJV). And if we know God hears us, we also know God will grant us the "petitions that we have asked of Him" (v. 15). We can have "confidence" God hears and answers our prayers (v. 14).

It may sound as if God has provided a blank check to the Christian . . . Though there is one important qualification: our requests must be "according to His will" (v. 14). If you are truly following Jesus with your whole heart, your desires in prayer will only be in accordance with God's plan and purpose for your life.

Prayer, therefore, . . . is ensuring our will lines up with God's purposes and then asking that His "will be done, on earth as it is in heaven" (Matthew 6:10).

—From *God Is Faithful*

GOD'S WORDS FOR YOU, GRANDMA

Do not throw away your confidence; it will be richly rewarded.

HEBREWS 10:35

The fruit of that righteousness will be peace; its effect will be quietness and confidence forever.

ISAIAH 32:17

We say with confidence, "The Lord is my helper; I will not be afraid. What can mere mortals do to me?"

HEBREWS 13:6

Let us . . . approach God's throne of grace with confidence, so that we may receive mercy and find grace to help us in our time of need.

HEBREWS 4:16

"I know that my redeemer lives, and that in the end he will stand on the earth."

JOB 19:25

I can do all this through him who gives me strength.

PHILIPPIANS 4:13

Truly he is my rock and my salvation; he is my fortress, I will never be shaken.

PSALM 62:2

I know whom I have believed, and am convinced that he is able to guard what I have entrusted to him until that day.

2 TIMOTHY 1:12

[God] who began a good work in you will carry it on to completion until the day of Christ Jesus.

PHILIPPIANS 1:6

This is the confidence we have in approaching God: that if we ask anything according to his will, he hears us.

1 JOHN 5:14

If our hearts do not condemn us, we have confidence before God.

1 JOHN 3:21

"The eternal God is your refuge, and underneath are the everlasting arms."

DEUTERONOMY 33:27

May the God who gives endurance and encouragement give you the same attitude of mind toward each other that Christ Jesus had, so that with one mind and one voice you may glorify the God and Father of our Lord Jesus Christ.

ROMANS 15:5–6

8

VERBAL ARROWS

Conflict is inevitable. Even the most loving of couples and devoted of friends will sometimes find themselves pulled apart by differences of background and belief. Such moments are dangerous. When emotions run high, the verbal arrows fly and lodge in places where they were never aimed.

We can avoid the danger of conflict by following one simple guideline: attack problems. Instead of focusing on the person with whom we're in conflict, we can direct our attention toward the problem that is separating us. Here are several helpful steps:

First, write your feelings down before you say them. Pour them out on paper. Second, define the problem. Start with several sentences, then whittle them down to a word or two that sums up the issue. Third, communicate the problem carefully. Resist saying "You always . . ." or "You never . . ." Avoid accusations and name-calling.

When we train ourselves to attack problems rather than people, we work our way toward healthy resolution without leaving casualties in our wake.

—Elisa Morgan

GOD'S WORDS FOR YOU, GRANDMA

Agree with one another in what you say [so] that there be no divisions among you.

1 CORINTHIANS 1:10

Hatred stirs up conflict, but love covers over all wrongs.

PROVERBS 10:12

Make every effort to keep the unity of the Spirit through the bond of peace.

EPHESIANS 4:3

Make sure that nobody pays back wrong for wrong.

1 THESSALONIANS 5:15

Do not be overcome by evil, but overcome evil with good.

ROMANS 12:21

Fools show their annoyance at once, but the prudent overlook an insult.

PROVERBS 12:16

It is to one's honor to avoid strife.

PROVERBS 20:3

Starting a quarrel is like breaching a dam; so drop the matter before a dispute breaks out.

PROVERBS 17:14

Where there is strife, there is pride, but wisdom is found in those who take advice.

PROVERBS 13:10

A gentle answer turns away wrath.

PROVERBS 15:1

Do not be quickly provoked in your spirit.

ECCLESIASTES 7:9

Whoever pursues righteousness and love finds life, prosperity and honor.

PROVERBS 21:21

"I will help you speak and will teach you what to say."

EXODUS 4:12

Lips that speak knowledge are a rare jewel.

PROVERBS 20:15

The boundary lines have fallen

for me in pleasant places;

surely I have a delightful inheritance.

PSALM 16:6

9

LIVES OF INCREASING

It is not without significance that Paul said, "*I have learned* to be content whatever the circumstances" (Philippians 4:11, italics added). He did not say, "I have always been content with any circumstances." For him, as it will be for us, it had been a painful learning process. The point is that he graduated!

Our Lord likened the Christian life to a river that broadened as it flowed down to the sea—an encouraging picture for the aging Christian. There is no reason why our lives now should not be as enjoyable, stimulating, and fruitful as they were earlier. Lives of increasing instead of diminishing, lives of continual outflow, can be ours.

Read again Christ's alluring picture: "Whoever believes in me, as Scripture has said, rivers of living water will flow from within them" (John 7:38). Such people refuse to concede defeat to Father Time. They resolve to master old age, not be defeated by it. They are grateful, thoughtful, cheerful, and content. Their very resilience is a great encouragement to their contemporaries who are incited to discover their secret.

—J. Oswald Sanders

GOD'S WORDS FOR YOU, GRANDMA

Better a small serving of vegetables with love than a fattened calf with hatred.

PROVERBS 15:17

Each person should live as a believer in whatever situation the Lord has assigned to them, just as God has called them.

1 CORINTHIANS 7:17

Godliness with contentment is great gain. For we brought nothing into the world, and we can take nothing out of it. But if we have food and clothing, we will be content with that.

1 TIMOTHY 6:6–8

Go, eat your food with gladness, and drink your wine with a joyful heart, for God has already approved what you do.

ECCLESIASTES 9:7

The cheerful heart has a continual feast.

PROVERBS 15:15

Better one handful with tranquility than two handfuls with toil and chasing after the wind.

ECCLESIASTES 4:6

A happy heart makes the face cheerful.

PROVERBS 15:13

Give me neither poverty nor riches, but give me only my daily bread.

PROVERBS 30:8

Better a little with the fear of the Lord than great wealth with turmoil.

PROVERBS 15:16

Better a little with righteousness than much gain with injustice.

PROVERBS 16:8

Better a dry crust with peace and quiet than a house full of feasting, with strife.

PROVERBS 17:1

God is our refuge and strength,

an ever-present help in trouble.

Therefore we will not fear,

though the earth give way

and the mountains fall into

the heart of the sea,

though its waters roar and foam

and the mountains quake

with their surging.

PSALM 46:1-3

10

SAME LAND. SAME GIANTS.

Discouragement and disappointment are like twins. Open the door to disappointment, and you will find discouragement dashing in right behind. Satan's goal is to dishearten you, to make you lose courage. Once discouragement enters your camp, it seems to be downhill all the way.

That is why God was so careful in His instructions to Joshua as the Israelites prepared to occupy the land that God had given them. They had missed occupying Canaan because of unbelief at Kadesh Barnea. Some forty years later, they were preparing to enter the same land and meet the same giants. So God said, not once but three times, "Be strong and courageous" (Joshua 1:6, 7, 9).

Yet they would not listen. Word of the giants and the fortified cities had penetrated their line of defense. Discouragement followed, bringing dejection and despair, until they were totally demoralized.

What is God's word to you today? It is to be strong and courageous, for your Father, the Lord God Omnipotent, reigns. Stop weeping and rejoice in the God of your salvation. He is your strength and He will enable you to stand (Habakkuk 3:18–19).

—Kay Arthur

GOD'S WORDS FOR YOU, GRANDMA

The Lord is my light and my salvation—whom shall I fear? The Lord is the stronghold of my life—of whom shall I be afraid?

PSALM 27:1

Wait for the Lord; be strong and take heart and wait for the Lord.

PSALM 27:14

Strengthen the feeble hands, steady the knees that give way; say to those with fearful hearts,

"Be strong, do not fear; your God will come."

ISAIAH 35:3–4

Because the hand of the Lord my God was on me, I took courage.

EZRA 7:28

"The Lord himself goes before you and will be with you; he will never leave you nor forsake you. Do not be afraid; do not be discouraged."

DEUTERONOMY 31:8

"Be strong and courageous, and do the work. Do not be afraid or discouraged, for the LORD God, my God, is with you. He will not fail you or forsake you."

1 CHRONICLES 28:20

Though I have fallen, I will rise. Though I sit in darkness, the LORD will be my light.

MICAH 7:8

The LORD is good to those whose hope is in him, to the one who seeks him.

LAMENTATIONS 3:25

I sought the LORD, and he answered me; he delivered me from all my fears.

PSALM 34:4

The LORD will be at your side and will keep your foot from being snared.

PROVERBS 3:26

"I have told you these things, so that in me you may have peace. In this world you will have trouble. But take heart! I have overcome the world."

JOHN 16:33

11

COME OPENLY TO HIM

It is one thing to feel loved by God when our life is together and all our support systems are in place. But what happens when we sin and fail, when our dreams shatter, when our investments crash, when we are regarded with suspicion? What happens when we come face-to-face with the human condition?

God calls us to come openly to Him. God is the Father who ran to His prodigal son when he came limping home. God loves who we really are—whether we like it or not. God calls us, as He did Adam (Genesis 3:8–9), to come out of hiding. No amount of spiritual makeup can render us more presentable to Him.

"Come to Me now," Jesus says. "Acknowledge and accept who I want to be for you: a Savior of boundless compassion, infinite patience, unbearable forgiveness, and love that keeps no score of wrongs. Quit projecting onto Me your own feelings about yourself. At this moment your life is a bruised reed and I will not crush it, a smoldering wick and I will not quench it. You are in a safe place."

—Brennan Manning

GOD'S WORDS FOR YOU, GRANDMA

Just as we share abundantly in the sufferings of Christ, so also our comfort abounds through Christ.

2 CORINTHIANS 1:5

Our present sufferings are not worth comparing with the glory that will be revealed in us.

ROMANS 8:18

We also glory in our sufferings, because we know that suffering produces perseverance; perseverance, character; and character, hope.

ROMANS 5:3–4

Consider it pure joy, my brothers and sisters, whenever you face trials of many kinds, because you know that the testing of your faith produces perseverance.

JAMES 1:2–3

For Christ's sake, I delight in weaknesses, in insults, in hardships, in persecutions, in difficulties. For when I am weak, then I am strong.

2 CORINTHIANS 12:10

The righteous person may have many troubles, but the Lord delivers him from them all.

PSALM 34:19

Blessed is the one who perseveres under trial because, having stood the test, that person will receive the crown of life that the Lord has promised to those who love him.

JAMES 1:12

You have been a refuge for the poor, a refuge for the needy in their distress, a shelter from the storm and a shade from the heat.

ISAIAH 25:4

The Spirit helps us in our weakness. We do not know what we ought to pray for, but the Spirit himself intercedes for us through wordless groans.

ROMANS 8:26

In the day of trouble he will keep me safe in his dwelling; he will hide me in the shelter of his sacred tent and set me high upon a rock.

PSALM 27:5

You have been my refuge, a strong tower against the foe. I long to dwell in your tent forever and take refuge in the shelter of your wings.

PSALM 61:3–4

All my longings lie open

before you, Lord;

my sighing is not hidden from you. . . .

Come quickly to help me,

my Lord and my Savior.

PSALM 38:9, 22

12

FILLED

As grandmothers, we may feel as if we're a cardboard juice box with fourteen straws stuck inside. Everyone comes and takes one draw and then another till we are bone-dry. And even when we are completely empty, we keep offering sips!

Why do we do this? Maybe we don't notice our dry condition. Maybe we believe we can push through anything. Maybe we've swallowed empty myths that say grandmothers aren't supposed to have needs. Whatever the reason, a drained grandma is an overreacting and overemotional grandma! When you're raising your voice too frequently, you know something is out of whack.

Jesus said, "Let anyone who is thirsty come to me and drink. Whoever believes in me, . . . rivers of living water will flow from within them" (John 7:37–38). Jesus was referring to the Holy Spirit, whom God installs in our souls when we come to know Him through Jesus.

Pull out the straws and line up your juice box opening to the faucet of God's fountain. Then do it again and again each day as you go about your grandmothering life. When you're filled, you'll be able to fill others.

—Elisa Morgan

GOD'S WORDS FOR YOU, GRANDMA

The mind governed by the Spirit is life and peace.

ROMANS 8:6

Put on the new self, which is being renewed in knowledge in the image of its Creator.

COLOSSIANS 3:10

Do not conform to the pattern of this world, but be transformed by the renewing of your mind.

ROMANS 12:2

"I will give you a new heart and put a new spirit in you; I will remove from you your heart of stone and give you a heart of flesh. And I will put my Spirit in you and move you to follow my decrees and be careful to keep my laws."

EZEKIEL 36:26–27

Search me, God, and know my heart; test me and know my anxious thoughts.

PSALM 139:23

Our mouths were filled with laughter, our tongues with songs of joy.

PSALM 126:2

How long must I wrestle with my thoughts and day after day have sorrow in my heart? . . . But I trust in your unfailing love; my heart rejoices in your salvation. I will sing the LORD's praise, for he has been good to me.

PSALM 13:2, 5-6

May the righteous be glad and rejoice before God; may they be happy and joyful.

PSALM 68:3

I will praise the LORD, who counsels me; even at night my heart instructs me. I keep my eyes always on the LORD. With him at my right hand, I will not be shaken. Therefore my heart is glad and my tongue rejoices.

PSALM 16:7-9

Is anyone happy? Let them sing songs of praise.

JAMES 5:13

I pour out before him my complaint; before him I tell my trouble. When my spirit grows faint within me, it is you who watch over my way.

PSALM 142:2-3

"When you pass through the waters,
I will be with you;
and when you pass through the rivers,
they will not sweep over you.
When you walk through the fire,
you will not be burned;
the flames will not set you ablaze."

ISAIAH 43:2

13

THE ROLE OF THE NURTURER

If you desire to influence another person, the way to start is by nurturing them. What clergyman John Knox said over four hundred years ago is still true: "You cannot antagonize and influence at the same time."

At the heart of the nurturing process is genuine concern for others. And as we try to help and influence the people around us, we must have positive feelings and concern for them. If you want to help people and make a positive impact on them, you cannot dislike or disparage them. You must give love to them and give them respect.

You may be wondering why you should take on a nurturing role with the people you want to influence, especially if they are employees, colleagues, or friends. You may be saying to yourself, "Isn't that something they can get somewhere else, like at home?" The unfortunate truth is that most people are desperate for encouragement. If you become a major nurturer in the life of another person, then you have an opportunity to make a major impact on them.

—John Maxwell

GOD'S WORDS FOR YOU, GRANDMA

Cast your cares on the LORD and he will sustain you; he will never let the righteous be shaken.

PSALM 55:22

In my alarm I said, "I am cut off from your sight!" Yet you heard my cry for mercy when I called to you for help.

PSALM 31:22

Truly my soul finds rest in God; my salvation comes from him.

PSALM 62:1

My soul is downcast within me. Yet this I call to mind and therefore I have hope: Because of the LORD's great love we are not consumed, for his compassions never fail. They are new every morning; great is your faithfulness.

LAMENTATIONS 3:20–23

Let the morning bring me word of your unfailing love, for I have put my trust in you. Show me the way I should go, for to you I entrust my life.

PSALM 143:8

My flesh and my heart may fail, but God is the strength of my heart and my portion forever.

PSALM 73:26

"I am the LORD your God who takes hold of your right hand and says to you, Do not fear; I will help you."

ISAIAH 41:13

He will show compassion, so great is his unfailing love.

LAMENTATIONS 3:32

In all their distress [the Lord] too was distressed, and the angel of his presence saved them. In his love and mercy he redeemed them; he lifted them up and carried them all the days of old.

ISAIAH 63:9

"I will refresh the weary and satisfy the faint."

JEREMIAH 31:25

"Let us acknowledge the LORD;

let us press on to acknowledge him.

As surely as the sun rises,

he will appear;

he will come to us like the winter rains."

HOSEA 6:3

14

A NEW STEP OF FAITH

You must admit, it was some kind of unorthodox military strategy: march around the city for six days without saying a word, on the seventh day go around seven times, listen for the long blast of the trumpet, and then shout.

Not exactly your ordinary procedure, but Joshua heard it in striking fashion from the commander of the Lord's army (Joshua 5:14), and he in turn passed it on to the people.

The Israelites followed God's instructions to a tee, even though the whole operation was a venture of faith that involved taking a tremendous risk. In the face of insurmountable odds, they relied on God's faithfulness. A nation notorious for its murmuring and complaining obeyed in silence. What a testimony to God's power.

Do you today face a personal Jericho—some unanswered prayer for family members or friends, some seemingly hopeless situation? Perhaps God is calling you today to a new step of faith, to a new risk-taking! The story of God's victory at Jericho rules out any hint of fatalism, which gives up hope because of high walls. It is God Himself who brings down the walls.

—Dirk R. Buursma

GOD'S WORDS FOR YOU, GRANDMA

Faith is confidence in what we hope for and assurance about what we do not see.

HEBREWS 11:1

Faith comes from hearing the message, and the message is heard through the word about Christ.

ROMANS 10:17

Abram believed the LORD, and he credited it to him as righteousness.

GENESIS 15:6

"Truly I tell you, if you have faith as small as a mustard seed, you can say to this mountain, 'Move from here to there,' and it will move. Nothing will be impossible for you."

MATTHEW 17:20

By faith we understand that the universe was formed at God's command, so that what is seen was not made out of what was visible.

HEBREWS 11:3

We live by faith, not by sight.

2 CORINTHIANS 5:7

It is by grace you have been saved, through faith—and this is not from yourselves, it is the gift of God—not by works, so that no one can boast.

EPHESIANS 2:8–9

Since we have been justified through faith, we have peace with God through our Lord Jesus Christ.

ROMANS 5:1

This righteousness is given through faith in Jesus Christ to all who believe.

ROMANS 3:22

The promise [of salvation] comes by faith, so that it may be by grace and may be guaranteed.

ROMANS 4:16

God has given us eternal life, and this life is in his Son. Whoever has the Son has life.

1 JOHN 5:11–12

In Christ Jesus you are all children of God through faith.

GALATIANS 3:26

From everlasting to everlasting

the LORD's love is with

those who fear him,

and his righteousness with

their children's children.

PSALM 103:17

15

THE SOLIDARITY OF FAMILY

God loves older people, and He has created them with inherent dignity. But another side of the dignity and worth of old age comes more specifically from a Christian understanding of the world. Christians understand the existence of another world, the world of God's love, toward which or against which our lives are being shaped. If you believe in this other world, it is not very hard to see that old age is meant to prepare us for it. So much that will be valueless there becomes, already, valueless here—independence, pride, wealth. So much that the kingdom of love depends on becomes already vitally necessary—interdependence, kindness, humility.

These qualities are usually expressed in families. To a remarkable degree, children and other relatives do get involved. While other relationships may shrivel to almost nothing, family relationships often grow stronger.

In that interlocking of parents and children, part of the goodness of old age reveals itself. You see the solidarity of human beings of all ages, a solidarity expressed concretely by the family. We really are in this together.

—Tim Stafford

GOD'S WORDS FOR YOU, GRANDMA

"A man will leave his father and mother and be united to his wife, and the two will become one flesh."

EPHESIANS 5:31

All your children will be taught by the LORD, and great will be their peace.

ISAIAH 54:13

"Whatever you did for one of the least of these brothers and sisters of mine, you did for me."

MATTHEW 25:40

As we have opportunity, let us do good to all people, especially to those who belong to the family of believers.

GALATIANS 6:10

Both the one who makes people holy and those who are made holy are of the same family. So Jesus is not ashamed to call them brothers and sisters.

HEBREWS 2:11

When you were dead in your sins and in the uncircumcision of your flesh, God made you alive with Christ. He forgave us all our sins, having canceled the charge of our legal indebtedness, which stood against us and condemned us; he has taken it away, nailing it to the cross.

COLOSSIANS 2:13–14

He has rescued us from the dominion of darkness and brought us into the kingdom of the Son he loves, in whom we have redemption, the forgiveness of sins.

COLOSSIANS 1:13–14

The Lord our God is merciful and forgiving, even though we have rebelled against him.

DANIEL 9:9

Who is a God like you, who pardons sin and forgives the transgression of the remnant of his inheritance? You do not stay angry forever but delight to show mercy.

MICAH 7:18

If we walk in the light, as he is in the light, we have fellowship with one another, and the blood of Jesus, his Son, purifies us from all sin. . . . If we confess our sins, he is faithful and just and will forgive us our sins and purify us from all unrighteousness.

1 JOHN 1:7, 9

Lord, hear my voice.
Let your ears be attentive
to my cry for mercy.
If you, LORD, kept a record of sins,
Lord, who could stand?
But with you there is forgiveness,
so that we can, with reverence, serve you.
I wait for the LORD, my
whole being waits,
and in his word I put my hope.

PSALM 130:2–5

16

THE BASIS OF LOVE

Tears came to her eyes as she read the letter. It was from a friend of her son, yes, her son who had run out of her life so many years ago. Abandoned her.

Her son's friend told how her son had been pursued and captured by the Lord, the same Lord who had changed her life. He wanted to come back now, to make it right again. In fact, he was coming back today. Today!

The pain he's put me through. I just don't know if I can forgive him. I want him to feel my pain and keep on feeling it all the days of his life. Why should I forgive him? He doesn't deserve it!

There was a knock at the door. Trembling with emotion, she opened it. The face—she had not seen the face for so long. The memories of rejection, pain, despair came flooding back. Then she remembered the letter she had just read: "I appeal to you on the basis of love . . . welcome him."

O Lord, I just don't know if I can forgive him. Please forgive me, Lord, forgive me. And at that moment, in the power of feeling forgiven, she reached out her arms—and welcomed him back.

—Dirk R. Buursma

GOD'S WORDS FOR YOU, GRANDMA

As far as the east is from the west, so far has he removed our transgressions from us.

PSALM 103:12

"I will cleanse them from all the sin they have committed against me and will forgive all their sins of rebellion against me."

JEREMIAH 33:8

Bear with each other and forgive one another if any of you has a grievance against someone. Forgive as the Lord forgave you.

COLOSSIANS 3:13

In him we have redemption through his blood, the forgiveness of sins, in accordance with the riches of God's grace that he lavished on us.

EPHESIANS 1:7–8

"Come now, let us settle the matter," says the Lord. "Though your sins are like scarlet, they shall be as white as snow; though they are red as crimson, they shall be like wool."

ISAIAH 1:18

"I, even I, am he who blots out your transgressions, for my own sake, and remembers your sins no more."

ISAIAH 43:25

God was reconciling the world to himself in Christ, not counting people's sins against them. And he has committed to us the message of reconciliation.

2 CORINTHIANS 5:19

He has reconciled you by Christ's physical body through death to present you holy in his sight, without blemish and free from accusation.

COLOSSIANS 1:22

Blessed is the one whose transgressions are forgiven, whose sins are covered. Blessed is the one whose sin the LORD does not count against them and in whose spirit is no deceit.

PSALM 32:1–2

Peter came to Jesus and asked, "Lord, how many times shall I forgive my brother or sister who sins against me? Up to seven times?" Jesus answered, "I tell you, not seven times, but seventy-seven times."

MATTHEW 18:21–22

Be kind and compassionate to one another, forgiving each other, just as in Christ God forgave you.

EPHESIANS 4:32

"Greater love has no one than this: to lay down one's life for one's friends. You are my friends if you do what I command. I no longer call you servants, because a servant does not know his master's business. Instead, I have called you friends."

JOHN 15:13–15

17

SOLIDIFY THE BRIDGES

A nation's strength is measured by the premium it puts on its own people. When people value people, an impenetrable web is drawn, a web of vitality and security.

A relationship. The delicate fusion of two human beings. The intricate weaving of two lives; two sets of moods, mentalities, and temperaments. Two intermingling hearts, both seeking solace and security.

A relationship. It has more power than any nuclear bomb and more potential than any promising seed. What matters most in life is not what we accumulate. What matters most is a relationship.

What steps are you taking to protect your "possessions"? What measure are you using to ensure that your relationships are strong and healthy? What are you doing to solidify the bridges between you and those in your world?

It's a wise [woman] who values people above possessions. Many wealthy people have died paupers because they gave their lives to things and not to people. And many paupers have left this earth in contentment because they loved their neighbors.

—Max Lucado

GOD'S WORDS FOR YOU, GRANDMA

One who has unreliable friends soon comes to ruin, but there is a friend who sticks closer than a brother.

PROVERBS 18:24

Perfume and incense bring joy to the heart, and the pleasantness of a friend springs from their heartfelt advice.

PROVERBS 27:9

Be devoted to one another in love. Honor one another above yourselves.

ROMANS 12:10

If we walk in the light, as he is in the light, we have fellowship with one another.

1 JOHN 1:7

"Anyone who withholds kindness from a friend forsakes the fear of the Almighty."

JOB 6:14

Be perfectly united in mind and thought.

1 CORINTHIANS 1:10

"My intercessor is my friend as my eyes pour out tears to God."

JOB 16:20

Let no debt remain outstanding, except the continuing debt to love one another.

ROMANS 13:8

A friend loves at all times, and a brother is born for a time of adversity.

PROVERBS 17:17

One who loves a pure heart and who speaks with grace will have the king for a friend.

PROVERBS 22:11

"Where you go I will go, and where you stay I will stay. Your people will be my people and your God my God. Where you die I will die, and there I will be buried. May the LORD deal with me, be it ever so severely, if even death separates you and me."

RUTH 1:16–17

Wounds from a friend can be trusted.

PROVERBS 27:6

Everyone who calls on the name of the Lord will be saved.

ROMANS 10:13

"For I know the plans I have for you," declares the LORD, "plans to prosper you and not to harm you, plans to give you hope and a future."

JEREMIAH 29:11

18

SAFELY IN GOD'S PRESENCE

The Bible tells us there can be hope for the future. First, there is hope of a changed person. No matter how hard we try, we are incapable of ridding ourselves of the selfishness and greed that cause conflict and strife and war. Our only hope is a changed heart—and Jesus is in the business of changing hearts.

Second, there is hope of a changed world. When we know Christ, He gives us by His Spirit a new love and concern for others. We can no longer be indifferent to their sufferings, and we'll want to do something about them. Changed by Christ, we can begin to change our world.

Third, there is hope of an unchanging eternity in Heaven. This world is not all there is. Someday all its pain and heartache will come to an end for those who know Christ (Revelation 21:4). Evil and death will be abolished, and we will be safely in God's presence forever.

As you read the headlines or look at your own life, you may be wondering if there is any hope. The answer from the Bible is a resounding yes.

—Billy Graham

GOD'S WORDS FOR YOU, GRANDMA

"My Father's will is that everyone who looks to the Son and believes in him shall have eternal life, and I will raise them up at the last day."

JOHN 6:40

"I give them eternal life, and they shall never perish; no one will snatch them out of my hand."

JOHN 10:28

Consider the blameless, observe the upright; a future awaits those who seek peace.

PSALM 37:37

"I say to all of you: From now on you will see the Son of Man sitting at the right hand of the Mighty One and coming on the clouds of heaven."

MATTHEW 26:64

"Consecrate yourselves, for tomorrow the LORD will do amazing things among you."

JOSHUA 3:5

I am convinced that neither death nor life, neither angels nor demons, neither the present nor the future, nor any powers, neither height nor depth, nor anything else in all creation, will be able to separate us from the love of God that is in Christ Jesus our Lord.

ROMANS 8:38–39

"In the beginning, Lord, you laid the foundations of the earth, and the heavens are the work of your hands. They will perish, but you remain; they will all wear out like a garment. You will roll them up like a robe; like a garment they will be changed. But you remain the same, and your years will never end."

HEBREWS 1:10–12

Know also that wisdom is like honey for you: If you find it, there is a future hope for you, and your hope will not be cut off.

PROVERBS 24:14

"The LORD will guide you always; he will satisfy your needs in a sun-scorched land and will strengthen your frame. You will be like a well-watered garden, like a spring whose waters never fail."

ISAIAH 58:11

There is now no condemnation for those who are in Christ Jesus.

ROMANS 8:1

"Give, and it will be given to you. A good measure, pressed down, shaken together and running over, will be poured into your lap. For with the measure you use, it will be measured to you."

LUKE 6:38

19

GENUINE FAITH

A true disciple of Jesus is a giver. Not just any kind of a giver, but a generous giver! The motivation for the believer should always be the example demonstrated by our Savior, Jesus Christ. Just as Jesus gave of Himself to meet our spiritual needs, we should always be quick to give generously to meet the needs of others.

When the apostle Paul wrote to the Corinthians, the Jerusalem church was experiencing deep poverty. The Corinthian believers had promised to give to help alleviate some of the Jerusalem believers' pain. Paul admonished them to be generous. He wanted their generosity to prove their faith.

The Corinthians gave joyfully to assist those in need, and their giving brought tremendous results. Jewish believers who had been skeptical of the Gentiles' faith saw by their actions that their faith was genuine. These Jewish believers also knew heartfelt gratitude to God for those who, in the spirit of Christ, had helped meet their needs. God was glorified.

As the Corinthians obeyed God by generously giving, they proclaimed the life-changing power of the gospel.

How good a giver are you?

—From *God Is Faithful*

GOD'S WORDS FOR YOU, GRANDMA

"Bring the whole tithe into the storehouse, that there may be food in my house. Test me in this," says the Lord Almighty, "and see if I will not throw open the floodgates of heaven and pour out so much blessing that there will not be room enough to store it."

MALACHI 3:10

"Store up for yourselves treasures in heaven, where moths and vermin do not destroy, and where thieves do not break in and steal. For where your treasure is, there your heart will be also."

MATTHEW 6:20–21

"It is more blessed to give than to receive."

ACTS 20:35

God is not unjust; he will not forget your work and the love you have shown him as you have helped his people and continue to help them.

HEBREWS 6:10

Do not forget to do good and to share with others, for with such sacrifices God is pleased.

HEBREWS 13:16

"Freely you have received; freely give."

MATTHEW 10:8

"When he, the Spirit of truth, comes, he will guide you into all the truth. He will not speak on his own; he will speak only what he hears, and he will tell you what is yet to come."

JOHN 16:13

I will instruct you and teach you in the way you should go; I will counsel you with my loving eye on you.

PSALM 32:8

"In your unfailing love you will lead the people you have redeemed. In your strength you will guide them to your holy dwelling."

EXODUS 15:13

Search me, God, and know my heart; test me and know my anxious thoughts. See if there is any offensive way in me, and lead me in the way everlasting.

PSALM 139:23–24

Whether you turn to the right or to the left, your ears will hear a voice behind you, saying, "This is the way; walk in it."

ISAIAH 30:21

He will cover you with his feathers,

and under his wings you

will find refuge;

his faithfulness will be your

shield and rampart.

PSALM 91:4

20

THE BEST THING TO COME

Because he delights in me, he saved me" (Psalm 18:19 NCV).

And you thought He saved you because of your decency. You thought He saved you because of your good works or good attitude or good looks. Sorry. If that were the case, your salvation would be lost when your voice went south or your works got weak. There are many reasons God saves you: to bring glory to Himself, to appease His justice, to demonstrate His sovereignty. But one of the sweetest reasons God saved you is because He is fond of you. He likes having you around. He thinks you are the best thing to come down the pike in quite a while. "As a man rejoices over his new wife, so your God will rejoice over you" (Isaiah 62:5 NCV).

If God had a refrigerator, your picture would be on it. If He had a wallet, your photo would be in it. He sends you flowers every spring and a sunrise every morning. Whenever you want to talk, He'll listen. He can live anywhere in the universe, and He chose your heart. And the Christmas gift He sent you in Bethlehem? Face it, friend. He's crazy about you.

—Max Lucado

GOD'S WORDS FOR YOU, GRANDMA

God is faithful, who has called you into fellowship with his Son, Jesus Christ our Lord.

1 CORINTHIANS 1:9

He is the Rock, his works are perfect, and all his ways are just. A faithful God who does no wrong, upright and just is he.

DEUTERONOMY 32:4

LORD, you are my God; I will exalt you and praise your name, for in perfect faithfulness you have done wonderful things, things planned long ago.

ISAIAH 25:1

The LORD is good and his love endures forever; his faithfulness continues through all generations.

PSALM 100:5

Let us hold unswervingly to the hope we profess, for he who promised is faithful.

HEBREWS 10:23

Praise be to the LORD, for he showed me the wonders of his love.

PSALM 31:21

He is the faithful God, keeping his covenant of love to a thousand generations of those who love him and keep his commandments.

DEUTERONOMY 7:9

"God is not human, that he should lie, not a human being, that he should change his mind. Does he speak and then not act? Does he promise and not fulfill?"

NUMBERS 23:19

The Lord is faithful, and he will strengthen you and protect you from the evil one.

2 THESSALONIANS 3:3

"To the faithful you show yourself faithful, to the blameless you show yourself blameless."

2 SAMUEL 22:26

"In all that has happened to us, you have remained righteous; you have acted faithfully."

NEHEMIAH 9:33

We love because he first loved us.

1 JOHN 4:19

"In your unfailing love you will lead the people you have redeemed."

EXODUS 15:13

To those who have been called, who are loved in God the Father and kept for Jesus Christ: Mercy, peace and love be yours in abundance.

JUDE VV. 1-2

21

BOUNTIFUL HARVEST

It is often into broken ground that the seeds of spring are planted; they germinate to grow into a bountiful harvest. And it is into broken hearts that God, in love, plants His Word to save and prepare His people for some great work. . . . Who can describe or measure the love of God? When we read of God's justice, it is justice tempered with love. When we read of God's righteousness, it is righteousness founded on love. When we read of God's atonement for sin, it is atonement necessitated because of His love, provided by His love, finished by His love.

When we read about the resurrection of Christ, we see the miracle of His love. When we read about the abiding presence of Christ, we know the power of His love. When we read about the return of Christ, we long for the fulfillment of His love.

No matter how black, dirty, shameful, or terrible our sin, God will forgive. We may be at the very gate of hell itself, but He will be reaching out in everlasting love.

—Billy Graham

GOD'S WORDS FOR YOU, GRANDMA

I am convinced that neither death nor life, neither angels nor demons, neither the present nor the future, nor any powers, neither height nor depth, nor anything else in all creation, will be able to separate us from the love of God that is in Christ Jesus our Lord.

ROMANS 8:38–39

Your love, LORD, reaches to the heavens, your faithfulness to the skies.

PSALM 36:5

According to your love remember me, for you, LORD, are good.

PSALM 25:7

See what great love the Father has lavished on us, that we should be called children of God! And that is what we are!

1 JOHN 3:1

How priceless is your unfailing love, O God! People take refuge in the shadow of your wings.

PSALM 36:7

I will sing of the Lord's great love forever; with my mouth I will make your faithfulness known through all generations.

PSALM 89:1

God demonstrates his own love for us in this: While we were still sinners, Christ died for us.

ROMANS 5:8

I pray that you, being rooted and established in love, may have power, together with all the Lord's holy people, to grasp how wide and long and high and deep is the love of Christ.

EPHESIANS 3:17–18

For God so loved the world that he gave his one and only Son, that whoever believes in him shall not perish but have eternal life.

JOHN 3:16

This is love: not that we loved God, but that he loved us and sent his Son as an atoning sacrifice for our sins.

1 JOHN 4:10

You, Lord, are forgiving and good, abounding in love to all who call to you.

PSALM 86:5

From everlasting to everlasting

the LORD's love is with those

who fear him,

and his righteousness

with their children's children—

with those who keep his covenant

and remember to obey his precepts.

PSALM 103:17–18

22

WHOLLY PERFECT

I am looking at a picture received yesterday of my latest grandchild—a picture taken the very day of his birth. I have many happy and grateful thoughts as I gaze at it, but beneath them all is a wonderment amounting to awe.

Here he is, this little man, every feature and organ intact and in place, the intricately balanced whole perfectly adapted to his intricately complicated new environment. In the wildest flight of fancy can we conceive of a miracle more miraculous than this? And yet no less amazing and inexplicable, no less wonderful is every common thing in our common life; and we should be able to see it so, if we were able to keep this baby's fresh, new eyes.

God reveals to babes what is hidden from the wise and prudent and that only to the extent we are able to turn, and become like little children, is it given us to see the kingdom of God.

—John Knox

GOD'S WORDS FOR YOU, GRANDMA

May the Lord bless you from Zion;
may you see the prosperity of Jerusalem
all the days of your life.
May you live to see your children's children.

PSALM 128:5-6

Children's children are a crown to the aged,
and parents are the pride of their children.

PROVERBS 17:6

Children are a heritage from the Lord.

PSALM 127:3

I instruct you in the way of wisdom and lead you along straight paths. When you walk, your steps will not be hampered; when you run, you will not stumble.

PROVERBS 4:11-12

The way of fools seems right to them, but the wise listen to advice.

PROVERBS 12:15

"Let us go up to the mountain of the LORD, to the temple of the God of Jacob. He will teach us his ways, so that we may walk in his paths."

ISAIAH 2:3

This is what the LORD says: "Stand at the crossroads and look; ask for the ancient paths, ask where the good way is, and walk in it, and you will find rest for your souls."

JEREMIAH 6:16

Teach me to do your will, for you are my God; may your good Spirit lead me on level ground.

PSALM 143:10

Praise the LORD, my soul, and forget not all his benefits—who forgives all your sins and heals all your diseases.

PSALM 103:2–3

Even when I am old and gray,
do not forsake me, my God,
till I declare your power
to the next generation,
your mighty acts to all who are to come.

PSALM 71:18

23

NO DUPLICATION

Laps open and ready for watching post-nap cartoons. Eyes crinkling in response to cartwheels and somersaults across the backyard. Heads thrown back in laughter during tickle sessions. Checks hidden in birthday cards. Games played on tables still sticky from holiday baking. Walks, hand in hand, through the leaves in the park. Ice cream on cones, stacked scoop upon scoop, licked in unison on an outside bench. Wrinkly hands curled atop piano keys while others gather around to listen.

Grandparents—we all bring offerings that no other can duplicate: An offering of wisdom that comes from living a lifetime. An offering of patience hewn from trial. An offering of laughter learned through making the most of both prosperous and lean times. Indeed, we "still bear fruit in old age." We "stay fresh and green" no matter our age (Psalm 92:14)! Let's thank God for the gift of being a grandparent.

—Elisa Morgan

GOD'S WORDS FOR YOU, GRANDMA

The righteous will flourish like a palm tree, they will grow like a cedar of Lebanon; planted in the house of the Lord, they will flourish in the courts of our God. They will still bear fruit in old age, they will stay fresh and green.

PSALM 92:12–14

Whoever fears the Lord has a secure fortress, and for their children it will be a refuge.

PROVERBS 14:26

I will open my mouth with a parable; I will utter hidden things, things from of old—things we have heard and known, things our ancestors have told us. We will not hide them from their descendants; we will tell the next generation the praiseworthy deeds of the Lord, his power, and the wonders he has done.

PSALM 78:2–4

[Older women] can urge the younger women to love their husbands and children.

TITUS 2:4

"I will make a covenant of peace with them and rid the land of savage beasts so that they may live in the wilderness and sleep in the forests in safety. I will make them and the places surrounding my hill a blessing. I will send down showers in season; there will be showers of blessing. The trees will yield their fruit and the ground will yield its crops; the people will be secure in their land. They will know that I am the LORD."

EZEKIEL 34:25–27

Grace and peace to you from him who is, and who was, and who is to come.

REVELATION 1:4

Love and faithfulness meet together; righteousness and peace kiss each other.

PSALM 85:10

The God of peace will be with you.

PHILIPPIANS 4:9

If it is possible, as far as it depends on you, live at peace with everyone.

ROMANS 12:18

Peacemakers who sow in peace reap a harvest of righteousness.

JAMES 3:18

Give praise to the LORD,

proclaim his name;

make known among the

nations what he has done.

1 CHRONICLES 16:8

24

GIVING GOOD GIFTS

God is the source of every good gift. God has given us everything good to enjoy, including rain to make things grow, minerals to make the soil fertile, animals for food and clothing, and energy for industry and transportation. Everything we have is from Him.

Jesus said, "If you, then, though you are evil, know how to give good gifts to your children, how much more will your Father in heaven give good gifts to those who ask him!" (Matthew 7:11). Paul added, "For everything God created is good, and nothing is to be rejected if it is received with thanksgiving, because it is consecrated by the word of God and prayer" (1 Timothy 4:4–5).

Sadly, unbelievers don't acknowledge God's goodness, though they benefit from it every day. They attribute His providential care to luck or fate. They do not honor Him as God or give Him thanks (Romans 1:21).

How sad to see such ingratitude, yet how thrilling to know that the infinite God cares for us and supplies our every need. Don't ever take His provisions for granted! Look to Him daily and receive His gifts with a thankful heart.

—John F. MacArthur Jr.

GOD'S WORDS FOR YOU, GRANDMA

Give thanks in all circumstances; for this is God's will for you in Christ Jesus.

1 THESSALONIANS 5:18

Thanks be to God! He gives us the victory through our Lord Jesus Christ.

1 CORINTHIANS 15:57

I will give thanks to the LORD because of his righteousness; I will sing the praises of the name of the LORD Most High.

PSALM 7:17

Give thanks to the LORD, for he is good; his love endures forever. Let the redeemed of the LORD tell their story.

PSALM 107:1–2

Just as you received Christ Jesus as Lord, continue to live your lives in him, rooted and built up in him, strengthened in the faith as you were taught, and overflowing with thankfulness.

COLOSSIANS 2:6–7

Thanks be to God, who always leads us as captives in Christ's triumphal procession and uses us to spread the aroma of the knowledge of him everywhere.

2 CORINTHIANS 2:14

Let them give thanks to the Lord for his unfailing love and his wonderful deeds for mankind.

PSALM 107:21

You turned my wailing into dancing; you removed my sackcloth and clothed me with joy, that my heart may sing your praises and not be silent. Lord my God, I will praise you forever.

PSALM 30:11–12

Come, let us sing for joy to the Lord; let us shout aloud to the Rock of our salvation. Let us come before him with thanksgiving and extol him with music and song.

PSALM 95:1–2

Praise the Lord. I will extol the Lord with all my heart in the council of the upright and in the assembly. Great are the works of the Lord; they are pondered by all who delight in them.

PSALM 111:1–2

"The LORD will guide you always;

he will satisfy your needs in

a sun-scorched land

and will strengthen your frame.

You will be like a well-watered garden,

like a spring whose waters never fail."

ISAIAH 58:11

25

HEAR AND OBEY

God allows us, His children, to lay our burdens and cares on Him as we seek guidance about how to live life—His life—in such tumultuous times as these. I suggest prayer with four petitions:

1. Show me what resources I have.
2. What are my alternatives in this situation?
3. Guide me to the best option. Show me why I should choose it.
4. I trust you to show me what to do next. Thank You for Your never-failing kindness.

Life involves a series of choices. Because decision-making is such a routine part of life, I sometimes forget that every action I select affects the young imitator I'm grandparenting. I find that I often live by trial and error, and I need to learn instead to live by asking God to help me live skillfully. Guidance begins and ends with hearing and obeying God's commands.

—Elisa Morgan

GOD'S WORDS FOR YOU, GRANDMA

This God is our God for ever and ever; he will be our guide even to the end.

PSALM 48:14

Trust in the LORD with all your heart and lean not on your own understanding; in all your ways submit to him, and he will make your paths straight.

PROVERBS 3:5-6

This is what the LORD says—your Redeemer, the Holy One of Israel: "I am the LORD your God, who teaches you what is best for you, who directs you in the way you should go."

ISAIAH 48:17

Keep your father's command and do not forsake your mother's teaching. Bind them always on your heart; fasten them around your neck. When you walk, they will guide you; when you sleep, they will watch over you; when you awake, they will speak to you. For this command is a lamp, this teaching is a light, and correction and instruction are the way to life.

PROVERBS 6:20-23

Since you are my rock and my fortress, for the sake of your name lead and guide me.

PSALM 31:3

If any of you lacks wisdom, you should ask God, who gives generously to all without finding fault, and it will be given to you.

JAMES 1:5

Commit to the LORD whatever you do, and he will establish your plans.

PROVERBS 16:3

He guards the course of the just and protects the way of his faithful ones.

PROVERBS 2:8

"For I know the plans I have for you," declares the LORD, "plans to prosper you and not to harm you, plans to give you hope and a future."

JEREMIAH 29:11

Show me your ways, LORD, teach me your paths. Guide me in your truth and teach me, for you are God my Savior, and my hope is in you all day long.

PSALM 25:4-5

Praise the LORD, my soul,

and forget not all his benefits—

who forgives all your sins

and heals all your diseases,

who redeems your life from the pit

and crowns you with love

and compassion.

PSALM 103:2–4

26

ULTIMATE HEALING

If you are sick, cry out to Jesus!

He will heal you—instantly or gradually or ultimately.

He may heal you instantly. One word was enough for Him to banish demons, heal epilepsy, and raise the dead. He may do this for you.

Or He may heal you gradually. In the case of a blind man from Bethsaida, Jesus healed him in stages (Mark 8:22–26).

And don't forget the story of Lazarus. By the time Jesus reached the cemetery, Lazarus had been in the tomb four days. But Jesus called him out. Did Jesus heal Lazarus? Yes, dramatically, but not immediately (John 11:1–44).

Our highest hope, however, is in our ultimate healing. In heaven God will restore our bodies to their intended splendor. "We know that when He is revealed, we shall be like Him" (1 John 3:2 NKJV). God will turn your tomb into a womb out of which you will be born with a perfect body into a perfect world. In the meantime keep praying. *Father, You are good. I need help. Heal me.*

—Max Lucado

GOD'S WORDS FOR YOU, GRANDMA

Surely he took up our pain and bore our suffering, yet we considered him punished by God, stricken by him, and afflicted. But he was pierced for our transgressions, he was crushed for our iniquities; the punishment that brought us peace was on him, and by his wounds we are healed.

ISAIAH 53:4–5

Jesus went throughout Galilee, teaching in their synagogues, proclaiming the good news of the kingdom, and healing every disease and sickness among the people.

MATTHEW 4:23

Is anyone among you sick? Let them call the elders of the church to pray over them and anoint them with oil in the name of the Lord. And the prayer offered in faith will make the sick person well; the Lord will raise them up.

JAMES 5:14–15

Our citizenship is in heaven. And we eagerly await a Savior from there, the Lord Jesus Christ.

PHILIPPIANS 3:20

You restored me to health and let me live.

ISAIAH 38:16

I pray that you may enjoy good health and that all may go well with you, even as your soul is getting along well.

3 JOHN V. 2

"I will heal my people and will let them enjoy abundant peace and security."

JEREMIAH 33:6

Heal me, LORD, and I will be healed; save me and I will be saved, for you are the one I praise.

JEREMIAH 17:14

Pay attention to what I say; turn your ear to my words. Do not let them out of your sight, keep them within your heart; for they are life to those who find them and health to one's whole body.

PROVERBS 4:20-22

"He himself bore our sins" in his body on the cross, so that we might die to sins and live for righteousness; "by his wounds you have been healed."

1 PETER 2:24

"What no eye has seen, what no ear has heard, and what no human mind has conceived" . . . these are the things God has revealed to us by his Spirit.

1 CORINTHIANS 2:9-10

"My Father's house has many rooms; if that were not so, would I have told you that I am going there to prepare a place for you? And if I go and prepare a place for you, I will come back and take you to be with me that you also may be where I am."

JOHN 14:2–3

27

DOOR TO ETERNITY

John, the old visionary, was allowed to have a brief view through the door to eternity. In the last book of the Bible, he presented what he saw, but not in a logical discourse. He painted a picture for us. He showed us through his eyes.

He saw many things, but one thing stood out: the throne of God. That throne drew all of John's attention. The splendor was so overwhelming, and the glitter of something like a glass sea around the throne so blinding, that John actually could not see God. He saw only the shining reflection, which reminded him of diamonds. Even John's sanctified, inspired eye could not see God in a vision. So great is God's glory that no eye has ever seen Him.

That is the heart of what heaven will be like: we shall see God. We can only be still in amazement: to see God and not to be last, to see God and live. We shall never be weary of looking at Him, for we shall never see everything. We shall fall from one ecstasy into the next.

To enter heaven and to see Jesus; to enjoy the company of the Redeemer. When I think of that, a strong desire to be there gets hold of me.

—Cornelis Gilhuis

GOD'S WORDS FOR YOU, GRANDMA

God raised us up with Christ and seated us with him in the heavenly realms in Christ Jesus.

EPHESIANS 2:6

"See, I will create new heavens and a new earth. The former things will not be remembered, nor will they come to mind."

ISAIAH 65:17

In keeping with his promise we are looking forward to a new heaven and a new earth, where righteousness dwells.

2 PETER 3:13

The Lord himself will come down from heaven, with a loud command, with the voice of the archangel and with the trumpet call of God, and the dead in Christ will rise first. After that, we who are still alive and are left will be caught up together with them in the clouds to meet the Lord in the air. And so we will be with the Lord forever.

1 THESSALONIANS 4:16–17

"Look, I am coming soon! My reward is with me, and I will give to each person according to what they have done."

REVELATION 22:12

The angel showed me the river of the water of life, as clear as crystal, flowing from the throne of God and of the Lamb down the middle of the great street of the city.

REVELATION 22:1–2

The city does not need the sun or the moon to shine on it, for the glory of God gives it light, and the Lamb is its lamp. The nations will walk by its light, and the kings of the earth will bring their splendor into it. On no day will its gates ever be shut, for there will be no night there. The glory and honor of the nations will be brought into it. Nothing impure will ever enter it, nor will anyone who does what is shameful or deceitful, but only those whose names are written in the Lamb's book of life.

REVELATION 21:23–27

The angel said to me, "Write this: Blessed are those who are invited to the wedding supper of the Lamb!" And he added, "These are the true words of God."

REVELATION 19:9

The twenty-four elders fall down before him who sits on the throne and worship him who lives for ever and ever. They lay their crowns before the throne and say: "You are worthy, our Lord and God, to receive glory and honor and power, for you created all things, and by your will they were created and have their being."

REVELATION 4:10–11

We say with confidence,

"The Lord is my helper; I

will not be afraid.

What can mere mortals do to me?"

HEBREWS 13:6

28

NEVER TOO LATE

When we were younger, most of us earnestly sought to discover God's plan for our lives. Are we equally diligent in seeking His plan for our old age, or are we just drifting along with no definite aim or goal?

With more time to review the past, we may become discouraged as we recall opportunities missed, a lessening of zeal in God's service, a mediocre prayer life, or perhaps actual sins of which we have reason to be ashamed. It is at such moments of introspection that we need to turn our eyes outward and upward to our loving and understanding Father. Romans 5:20 says, "Where sin increased, grace increased all the more."

The wonderful thing about God's abundant grace and favor is that it is never too late to discover and follow God's plan for the remainder of our lives, never too late to make a new start.

To disillusioned compatriots, the prophet Joel brought an inspiring message of hope—the hope of a new beginning: "I will repay you for the years the locusts have eaten" (2:25).

—J. Oswald Sanders

GOD'S WORDS FOR YOU, GRANDMA

We have put our hope in the living God, who is the Savior of all people, and especially of those who believe.

1 TIMOTHY 4:10

Put your hope in the LORD both now and forevermore.

PSALM 131:3

Guide me in your truth and teach me, for you are God my Savior, and my hope is in you all day long.

PSALM 25:5

Hope does not put us to shame, because God's love has been poured out into our hearts through the Holy Spirit, who has been given to us.

ROMANS 5:5

Yes, my soul, find rest in God; my hope comes from him.

PSALM 62:5

Why, my soul, are you downcast? Why so disturbed within me? Put your hope in God, for I will yet praise him, my Savior and my God.

PSALM 42:11

Your hands made me and formed me; give me understanding to learn your commands. May those who fear you rejoice when they see me, for I have put my hope in your word.

PSALM 119:73–74

Yet this I call to mind and therefore I have hope: Because of the LORD's great love we are not consumed, for his compassions never fail. . . . The LORD is good to those whose hope is in him, to the one who seeks him.

LAMENTATIONS 3:21–22, 25

The eyes of the LORD are on those who fear him, on those whose hope is in his unfailing love.

PSALM 33:18

May your unfailing love be with us, LORD, even as we put our hope in you.

PSALM 33:22

Put your hope in the LORD, for with the LORD is unfailing love and with him is full redemption.

PSALM 130:7

May our Lord Jesus Christ himself and God our Father, who loved us and by his grace gave us eternal encouragement and good hope, encourage your hearts and strengthen you in every good deed and word.

2 THESSALONIANS 2:16–17

The Lord will rescue me from every evil attack and will bring me safely to his heavenly kingdom. To him be glory for ever and ever.

2 TIMOTHY 4:18

29

LOOK AHEAD

We who love the Lord are to hate sin. Indeed, the Christian life is a battle against it. That's why we are equipped to be soldiers (Ephesians 6). Sometimes the veterans get tired and decide to leave warfare to the young recruits. Fighting for truth and justice is wearying.

Moses was past eighty when he led the Israelites out of Egypt. The next forty years were full of fighting. Moses got weary. At 120 Moses was still warning the people about sin.

In Hebrews 11 it says, "He regarded disgrace for the sake of Christ as of greater value than the treasures of Egypt, because he was looking ahead to his reward" (v. 26). Looking ahead. Anticipating the day when he would be with the Lord.

When we feel like quitting—retiring or even going AWOL—let us remember Moses and look ahead. When we have fought the last battle, God stands ready to welcome us to eternal peace.

—Jean Shaw

GOD'S WORDS FOR YOU, GRANDMA

If anybody does sin, we have an advocate with the Father—Jesus Christ, the Righteous One.

1 JOHN 2:1

All have sinned and fall short of the glory of God, and all are justified freely by his grace through the redemption that came by Christ Jesus.

ROMANS 3:23-24

Through Christ Jesus the law of the Spirit who gives life has set you free from the law of sin and death.

ROMANS 8:2

We all, like sheep, have gone astray, each of us has turned to our own way; and the LORD has laid on him the iniquity of us all.

ISAIAH 53:6

Our struggle is not against flesh and blood, but against the rulers, against the authorities, against the powers of this dark world and against the spiritual forces of evil in the heavenly realms.

EPHESIANS 6:12

No temptation has overtaken you except what is common to mankind. And God is faithful; he will not let you be tempted beyond what you can bear. But when you are tempted, he will also provide a way out so that you can endure it.

1 CORINTHIANS 10:13

I acknowledged my sin to you and did not cover up my iniquity. I said, "I will confess my transgressions to the LORD." And you forgave the guilt of my sin.

PSALM 32:5

Count yourselves dead to sin but alive to God in Christ Jesus.

ROMANS 6:11

"The joy of the LORD is your strength."

NEHEMIAH 8:10

The LORD has done great things for us, and we are filled with joy.

PSALM 126:3

The precepts of the LORD are right, giving joy to the heart. The commands of the LORD are radiant, giving light to the eyes.

PSALM 19:8

Your statutes are my heritage forever; they are the joy of my heart.

PSALM 119:111

I delight greatly in the LORD;
my soul rejoices in my God.
For he has clothed me with
garments of salvation
and arrayed me in a robe
of his righteousness,
as a bridegroom adorns
his head like a priest,
and as a bride adorns
herself with her jewels.

ISAIAH 61:10

30

INVISIBLE REALITIES

We are deluged by the visible—a world in chaos, a nation divided, financial struggles, family problems, physical ailments. When our focus is limited to the visible, we grow frightened. But when we realize invisible realities are at play, we cannot lose heart. With spiritual eyes we see the Father, the Son, and the Holy Spirit. We see God's holy angels surrounding the earth. We trust in the qualities of God. We believe God's promises and wait with earnest expectation for their unstoppable fulfillment. And we yearn for heaven. These unseen realities are greater than the negative realities surrounding us. . . .

When you awaken each morning, envision God standing there to greet you. As you drive to work, speak to Him naturally, as if He were in the passenger seat. Before an appointment, whisper a prayer for His help. As you relax at the end of the day, your work behind you, remember the angels hovering near. As you turn down the covers of your bed, remember you are blanketed with the promises of God. As you fall asleep, ponder your heavenly home.

God is closer than you know, and His unseen grace will, in His timing, overturn all of life's unseemly moments.

—Robert J. Morgan

GOD'S WORDS FOR YOU, GRANDMA

Light shines on the righteous and joy on the upright in heart.

PSALM 97:11

His favor lasts a lifetime; weeping may stay for the night, but rejoicing comes in the morning.

PSALM 30:5

May all who seek you rejoice and be glad in you; may those who long for your saving help always say, "The Lord is great!"

PSALM 70:4

The righteous will rejoice in the Lord and take refuge in him; all the upright in heart will glory in him!

PSALM 64:10

Let all who take refuge in you be glad; let them ever sing for joy. Spread your protection over them, that those who love your name may rejoice in you.

PSALM 5:11

The prospect of the righteous is joy.

PROVERBS 10:28

Be glad, people of Zion, rejoice in the LORD your God, for he has given you the autumn rains because he is faithful. He sends you abundant showers, both autumn and spring rains, as before.

JOEL 2:23

"Until now you have not asked for anything in my name. Ask and you will receive, and your joy will be complete."

JOHN 16:24

Those the LORD has rescued will return. They will enter Zion with singing; everlasting joy will crown their heads. Gladness and joy will overtake them, and sorrow and sighing will flee away.

ISAIAH 51:11

The LORD your God will bless you in all your harvest and in all the work of your hands, and your joy will be complete.

DEUTERONOMY 16:15

You make known to me the path of life; you will fill me with joy in your presence, with eternal pleasures at your right hand.

PSALM 16:11

The kingdom of God is . . . righteousness, peace and joy in the Holy Spirit.

ROMANS 14:17

Nebuchadnezzar said, "Praise be to the God of Shadrach, Meshach and Abednego, who has sent his angel and rescued his servants! They trusted in him and defied the king's command and were willing to give up their lives rather than serve or worship any god except their own God."

DANIEL 3:28

31

STRONGER THAN DEATH

The resurrection is the expression of God's faithfulness to Jesus and to all God's children. Through the resurrection God has said to Jesus, "You are indeed My beloved Son, and My love is everlasting," and to us God has said, "You indeed are My beloved children, and My love is everlasting." The resurrection is God's way of revealing to us that nothing that belongs to God will ever go to waste. What belongs to God will never get lost.

The resurrection doesn't answer any of our curious questions about life after death, such as, How will it be? How will it look? But it does reveal to us that, indeed, love is stronger than death. After that revelation, we must remain silent, leave the whys, wheres, hows, and whens behind, and simply trust. . . .

As the father of the epileptic boy, who asked Jesus to heal his child, we will always have to say, "I do believe; help me overcome my unbelief!" (Mark 9:24). Still, when we keep our eyes fixed on the risen Lord, we may find not only that love is stronger than death but also that our faith is stronger than our skepticism.

—Henri J. M. Nouwen

GOD'S WORDS FOR YOU, GRANDMA

"Do not let your hearts be troubled. You believe in God; believe also in me."

JOHN 14:1

He has delivered us from such a deadly peril, and he will deliver us again. On him we have set our hope that he will continue to deliver us.

2 CORINTHIANS 1:10

Those who know your name trust in you, for you, LORD, have never forsaken those who seek you.

PSALM 9:10

Trust in the LORD forever, for the LORD, the LORD himself, is the Rock eternal.

ISAIAH 26:4

Those who trust in the LORD are like Mount Zion, which cannot be shaken but endures forever.

PSALM 125:1

It is better to take refuge in the Lord than to trust in humans. It is better to take refuge in the Lord than to trust in princes.

PSALM 118:8–9

Why, my soul, are you downcast? Why so disturbed within me? Put your hope in God, for I will yet praise him, my Savior and my God.

PSALM 42:5

Whoever gives heed to instruction prospers, and blessed is the one who trusts in the Lord.

PROVERBS 16:20

Those who trust in the Lord will prosper.

PROVERBS 28:25

Anyone who believes in him will never be put to shame.

ROMANS 10:11

Fear of man will prove to be a snare, but whoever trusts in the Lord is kept safe.

PROVERBS 29:25

When the kindness and love of God our Savior appeared, he saved us, not because of righteous things we had done, but because of his mercy.

TITUS 3:4–5

32

GOODNESS STANDS

A little girl was overheard praying, "Lord, make all the bad people good and all the good people nice." God wants His people to be good. But it isn't enough.

In addition to being good, we need to be kind. Planted by the God who is wholly good, the quality of goodness takes root within our hearts, growing all around and through our beliefs and motivations. Our kindness is then the fruitful expression on the outside of the goodness that has been cultivated within.

Goodness recognizes a shortage. Kindness provides for it. Goodness stands against hunger. Kindness sends money to the poor to buy food. Goodness knows that we are to care for the lonely. Kindness goes to the hospital with a lonely single mother and coaches her through labor and delivery. Goodness realizes there's a job to be done. Kindness does the job.

Dear Lord, please teach me to demonstrate goodness by being kind. Move me past the sidelines of concern to the arena of action. As You work in my life to make me good—more like You—please make me nice as well. Amen.

—Elisa Morgan

GOD'S WORDS FOR YOU, GRANDMA

Love is kind. It does not envy, it does not boast, it is not proud.

1 CORINTHIANS 13:4

Carry each other's burdens, and in this way you will fulfill the law of Christ.

GALATIANS 6:2

As we have opportunity, let us do good to all people.

GALATIANS 6:10

As God's chosen people, holy and dearly loved, clothe yourselves with compassion, kindness, humility, gentleness and patience.

COLOSSIANS 3:12

The fruit of the Spirit is love, joy, peace, forbearance, kindness, goodness, faithfulness.

GALATIANS 5:22

Make every effort to add to your faith . . . mutual affection; and to mutual affection, love. For if you possess these qualities in increasing measure, they will keep you from being ineffective and unproductive in your knowledge of our Lord Jesus Christ.

2 PETER 1:5, 7–8

[Ruth] bowed down with her face to the ground. She asked him, "Why have I found such favor in your eyes that you notice me—a foreigner?" Boaz replied, "I've been told all about what you have done for your mother-in-law since the death of your husband—how you left your father and mother and your homeland and came to live with a people you did not know before. May the LORD repay you for what you have done. May you be richly rewarded by the LORD, the God of Israel, under whose wings you have come to take refuge."

RUTH 2:10–12

If anyone has material possessions and sees a brother or sister in need but has no pity on them, how can the love of God be in that person? Dear children, let us not love with words or speech but with actions and in truth.

1 JOHN 3:17–18

"If anyone gives even a cup of cold water to one of these little ones who is my disciple, truly I tell you, that person will certainly not lose their reward."

MATTHEW 10:42

"In everything, do to others what you would have them do to you, for this sums up the Law and the Prophets."

MATTHEW 7:12

Be kind and compassionate to one another, forgiving each other, just as in Christ God forgave you.

EPHESIANS 4:32

33

ECHOES OF WISDOM

Jumping in with good advice is our natural reaction to any problem our grandchildren have. But resisting the urge to shower them with the benefit of our great wisdom is the sign of a good listener.

By taking the time to listen for feelings and echo back what we hear, we enable our grandchildren to see and understand more clearly what is going on in their lives. This helps them learn to take the steps necessary toward solving their own problems. By asking questions, you show them you are really attentive to what they are saying. Because this is a compliment to your grandchildren, their response is likely to come more readily.

Some of us are especially tempted to overwhelm our grandchildren with spiritual and scriptural answers, many of which can come across as frustratingly pat. Instead of listening to what the kids are saying, we spend our time watching for an opening where we can present our own point of view. There's nothing wrong with sharing your wisdom. It's an important part of teaching—if you wait for your grandchildren to ask for it and if you have listened enough to earn the right to share it.

—Jan Stoop and Betty Southard

GOD'S WORDS FOR YOU, GRANDMA

The Holy Spirit says: "Today, if you hear his voice, do not harden your hearts as you did in the rebellion, during the time of testing in the wilderness."

HEBREWS 3:7–8

Whoever heeds life-giving correction will be at home among the wise.

PROVERBS 15:31

"Everyone who has heard the Father and learned from him comes to me."

JOHN 6:45

"Here I am! I stand at the door and knock. If anyone hears my voice and opens the door, I will come in and eat with that person, and they with me."

REVELATION 3:20

I am convinced that neither death nor life, neither angels nor demons, neither the present nor the future, nor any powers, neither height nor depth, nor anything else in all creation, will be able to separate us from the love of God that is in Christ Jesus our Lord.

ROMANS 8:38–39

Come near to God and he will come near to you.

JAMES 4:8

Praise be to God, who has not rejected my prayer or withheld his love from me!

PSALM 66:20

I call to God, and the LORD saves me.

PSALM 55:16

"Do not fear, for I am with you; do not be dismayed, for I am your God. I will strengthen you and help you; I will uphold you with my righteous right hand."

ISAIAH 41:10

God has said, "Never will I leave you; never will I forsake you."

HEBREWS 13:5

The LORD said, "Go out and stand on the mountain in the presence of the LORD, for the LORD is about to pass by." Then a great and powerful wind tore the mountains apart and shattered the rocks before the LORD, but the LORD was not in the wind. After the wind there was an earthquake, but the LORD was not in the earthquake. After the earthquake came a fire, but the LORD was not in the fire. And after the fire came a gentle whisper. When Elijah heard it, he pulled his cloak over his face and went out and stood at the mouth of the cave.

1 KINGS 19:11-13

"Though the mountains be shaken

and the hills be removed,

yet my unfailing love for

you will not be shaken

nor my covenant of peace be removed,"

says the LORD, who has

compassion on you.

ISAIAH 54:10

34

GREATEST SOURCE

Many people remain lonely because they fear rejection. They think rejection hurts worse than loneliness and spend much of their time and money trying to avoid it. But that is a wrong attitude. Those who expect to be rejected usually will feel that they are. Those who expect to receive friendship and comfort usually will.

When you need friendship and comfort, offer friendship and comfort, and don't expect rejection. Accept yourself where you are, whatever your need, and remember that Christ will not reject you. When you reach out to Him, He will always respond with loving acceptance. He says in Matthew 7:11, "If you then, being evil, know how to give good gifts to your children [and your friends and all those around you], how much more will your Father who is in heaven give good things to those who ask Him!" (NKJV).

Your greatest source of comfort and hope is Christ Jesus.

—Dr. David Jeremiah

GOD'S WORDS FOR YOU, GRANDMA

In Christ we, though many, form one body, and each member belongs to all the others.

ROMANS 12:5

"Be strong and courageous. Do not be afraid or terrified because of them, for the LORD your God goes with you; he will never leave you nor forsake you."

DEUTERONOMY 31:6

I am always with you; you hold me by my right hand.

PSALM 73:23

"Surely I am with you always, to the very end of the age."

MATTHEW 28:20

"I will not leave you as orphans; I will come to you."

JOHN 14:18

At my first defense, no one came to my support, but everyone deserted me. May it not be held against them. But the Lord stood at my side and gave me strength.

2 TIMOTHY 4:16–17

"I am with you and will watch over you wherever you go. . . . I will not leave you until I have done what I have promised you."

GENESIS 28:15

"Do not let your hearts be troubled. You believe in God; believe also in me."

JOHN 14:1

Though my father and mother forsake me, the LORD will receive me.

PSALM 27:10

You are with me; your rod and your staff, they comfort me.

PSALM 23:4

May the Lord of peace himself give you peace at all times and in every way. The Lord be with all of you.

2 THESSALONIANS 3:16

The peace of God, which transcends all understanding, will guard your hearts and your minds in Christ Jesus.

PHILIPPIANS 4:7

He heals the brokenhearted and binds up their wounds.

PSALM 147:3

Live a life worthy of the Lord and please him in every way: bearing fruit in every good work, growing in the knowledge of God, being strengthened with all power according to his glorious might so that you may have great endurance and patience.

COLOSSIANS 1:10–11

35

WORKING IN THE WAIT

We wait for everything! For the dryer to finish. For our husbands to get home. For the phone to ring. For the pie to bake. For the mail to come. For a car to pull up, bringing our grandchildren for a visit. For a job. For answers to prayer.

With so much experience, we're remarkably unskilled at waiting well. Waiting seems to us a waste of time.

But the fact is that while we are waiting, God is working: To move us where He wants us to be. To readjust the lives of others so His ultimate desires will be fulfilled. To bring about what will make us eventually Christlike, though maybe not immediately comfortable.

What are you waiting for? And more to the point, how well are you waiting for it?

We must pray with a willingness to wait and wait with a willingness to pray. Waiting and praying go together. Like two shoes of a pair or two halves of a whole, they work as a team.

—Elisa Morgan

GOD'S WORDS FOR YOU, GRANDMA

Be still before the Lord and wait patiently for him; do not fret when people succeed in their ways, when they carry out their wicked schemes.

PSALM 37:7

Everyone should be quick to listen, slow to speak and slow to become angry.

JAMES 1:19

The end of a matter is better than its beginning, and patience is better than pride.

ECCLESIASTES 7:8

It is good to wait quietly for the salvation of the Lord.

LAMENTATIONS 3:26

Wait for the Lord; be strong and take heart and wait for the Lord.

PSALM 27:14

Lord, walking in the way of your laws, we wait for you; your name and renown are the desire of our hearts.

ISAIAH 26:8

Be joyful in hope, patient in affliction, faithful in prayer.

ROMANS 12:12

Love is patient.

1 CORINTHIANS 13:4

I wait for the LORD, my whole being waits, and in his word I put my hope. I wait for the Lord more than watchmen wait for the morning.

PSALM 130:5–6

Be patient with everyone.

1 THESSALONIANS 5:14

See how the farmer waits for the land to yield its valuable crop, patiently waiting for the autumn and spring rains. You too, be patient and stand firm, because the Lord's coming is near.

JAMES 5:7–8

If we hope for what we do not yet have, we wait for it patiently.

ROMANS 8:25

Be completely humble and gentle; be patient, bearing with one another in love.

EPHESIANS 4:2

"The LORD bless you

and keep you;

the LORD make his face shine on you

and be gracious to you;

the LORD turn his face toward you

and give you peace."

NUMBERS 6:24–26

36

MORNING JOY

Roaring winds, the spray of sleet and snow, dangerous and slippery ice. Remember those storms when you were a child? I sure do. I'd shiver under my quilt. Would the house survive? Would I? Moaning winds made me feel lonesome. Would morning ever come?

Yes, but with it, a different picture. I awoke to soft rays of sun warming my bed covers. Quiet called me out of bed and to the window where I gasped at the dazzling white landscape. It was beautiful.

There are days when my soul feels windblown, raw, and exposed—times when I'm tossed in a blustery tempest with everything breaking loose. But the God who brings beauty out of blizzards promises to bring peace after the storm. And when the beauty dawns, I hardly remember the fright of that stormy trial.

If you sense storm warnings, hold on to a couple of "winter watch" verses from Scripture. Recall how near and present the Lord really is. Remember that joy comes in the morning. Let Him cover your fear with His love, like a blanket of snow, soft and gentle. Cling to His promise of peace.

—Joni Eareckson Tada

GOD'S WORDS FOR YOU, GRANDMA

"Peace I leave with you; my peace I give you. I do not give to you as the world gives. Do not let your hearts be troubled and do not be afraid."

JOHN 14:27

In peace I will lie down and sleep, for you alone, LORD, make me dwell in safety.

PSALM 4:8

LORD, you establish peace for us; all that we have accomplished you have done for us.

ISAIAH 26:12

Grace and peace to you from God our Father and the Lord Jesus Christ.

PHILIPPIANS 1:2

You will keep in perfect peace those whose minds are steadfast, because they trust in you.

ISAIAH 26:3

Seek peace and pursue it.

PSALM 34:14

The fruit of that righteousness will be peace; its effect will be quietness and confidence forever.

ISAIAH 32:17

The LORD longs to be gracious to you; therefore he will rise up to show you compassion. For the LORD is a God of justice. Blessed are all who wait for him!

ISAIAH 30:18

Strive for full restoration, encourage one another, be of one mind, live in peace. And the God of love and peace will be with you.

2 CORINTHIANS 13:11

When the LORD takes pleasure in anyone's way, he causes their enemies to make peace with them.

PROVERBS 16:7

Great peace have those who love your law, and nothing can make them stumble.

PSALM 119:165

You know the message God sent to the people of Israel, announcing the good news of peace through Jesus Christ, who is Lord of all.

ACTS 10:36

This is the confidence we have in approaching God: that if we ask anything according to his will, he hears us. And if we know that he hears us—whatever we ask—we know that we have what we asked of him.

1 JOHN 5:14–15

37

BRAND-NEW DAY

At the end of every new day, the last thing I do is to have a prayer. "Father in heaven, Jesus Christ, I've sinned again today." And I try to think of what my sins are specifically. I confess. I ask God to forgive me. I know He does. He died on the cross for me.

Now, that's the first thing I pray for. Then I pray for His Spirit to come and fill my life. I know He does, so I sleep peacefully. If I wake up very, very early, it's because I'm enthused and excited about things I can do for God. Then I begin the day with this prayer: "Father in heaven, this morning is a brand-new day! Filled with bright new opportunities!" Isn't that exciting!

If you begin your day that way and if you end your day that way, chances are that in between you're going to have a lot of positive emotions, because the Holy Spirit of God will come into your life, guide you, lead you, and direct you. You're going to get involved, and that means you're going to get excited, and it also means you'll become enthused! And that means energy!

—Robert H. Schuller

GOD'S WORDS FOR YOU, GRANDMA

"Ask and it will be given to you; seek and you will find; knock and the door will be opened to you. For everyone who asks receives; the one who seeks finds; and to the one who knocks, the door will be opened."

MATTHEW 7:7–8

"I tell you that if two of you on earth agree about anything they ask for, it will be done for them by my Father in heaven. For where two or three gather in my name, there am I with them."

MATTHEW 18:19–20

Dear friends, if our hearts do not condemn us, we have confidence before God and receive from him anything we ask, because we keep his commands and do what pleases him.

1 JOHN 3:21–22

"You will call on me and come and pray to me, and I will listen to you. You will seek me and find me when you seek me with all your heart."

JEREMIAH 29:12–13

The Lord . . . hears the prayer of the righteous.

PROVERBS 15:29

Let all the faithful pray to you while you may be found; surely the rising of the mighty waters will not reach them.

PSALM 32:6

The LORD is near to all who call on him, to all who call on him in truth.

PSALM 145:18

Hear me, LORD, my plea is just; listen to my cry. Hear my prayer—it does not rise from deceitful lips.

PSALM 17:1

Answer me when I call to you, my righteous God. Give me relief from my distress; have mercy on me and hear my prayer.

PSALM 4:1

"Call to me and I will answer you and tell you great and unsearchable things you do not know."

JEREMIAH 33:3

"He will call on me, and I will answer him; I will be with him in trouble, I will deliver him and honor him."

PSALM 91:15

"I will do whatever you ask in my name, so that the Father may be glorified in the Son. You may ask me for anything in my name, and I will do it."

JOHN 14:13-14

"Let the beloved of the LORD
rest secure in him,
for he shields him all day long,
and the one the LORD loves
rests between his shoulders."

DEUTERONOMY 33:12

38

PERFECT REST

I knew a Christian lady who had a very heavy temporal burden. One day, she noticed a little tract called "Anna's Faith." She picked it up and began to read it. The story was of a poor woman who had been carried triumphantly through a life of unusual sorrow. She was giving the history of her life to a kind visitor, and the visitor said feelingly, "Oh, Anna, I do not see how you could bear so much sorrow!"

"I did not bear it," was the quick reply. "The Lord bore it for me."

"Yes," said the visitor, "that is the right way. We must take our troubles to the Lord."

"Yes," replied Anna, "but we must do more than that: we must leave them there. Most people take their burdens to Him, but they bring them away with them again. But I take mine and I leave them with Him, and come away and forget them. If the worry comes back, I take it to Him again; and I do this over and over, until at last I just forget I have any worries and am at perfect rest."

—Hannah Whitall Smith

GOD'S WORDS FOR YOU, GRANDMA

"Come to me, all you who are weary and burdened, and I will give you rest. Take my yoke upon you and learn from me, for I am gentle and humble in heart, and you will find rest for your souls."

MATTHEW 11:28–29

The LORD replied, "My Presence will go with you, and I will give you rest."

EXODUS 33:14

Whoever dwells in the shelter of the Most High will rest in the shadow of the Almighty.

PSALM 91:1

This is what the LORD says: "Stand at the crossroads and look; ask for the ancient paths, ask where the good way is, and walk in it, and you will find rest for your souls."

JEREMIAH 6:16

Return to your rest, my soul, for the LORD has been good to you.

PSALM 116:7

"Do not fear, for I am with you; do not be dismayed, for I am your God. I will strengthen you and help you; I will uphold you with my righteous right hand."

ISAIAH 41:10

"I will refresh the weary and satisfy the faint."

JEREMIAH 31:25

He makes me lie down in green pastures, he leads me beside quiet waters, he refreshes my soul. He guides me along the right paths for his name's sake.

PSALM 23:2–3

Because so many people were coming and going that they did not even have a chance to eat, [Jesus] said to them, "Come with me by yourselves to a quiet place and get some rest."

MARK 6:31

Take delight in the LORD, and he will give you the desires of your heart.

PSALM 37:4

"If my people, who are called by my name, will humble themselves and pray and seek my face and turn from their wicked ways, then I will hear from heaven, and I will forgive their sin and will heal their land."

2 CHRONICLES 7:14

Be sure to fear the LORD and serve him faithfully with all your heart; consider what great things he has done for you.

1 SAMUEL 12:24

39

SERVE WITH JOY

Delight in God's service is a sign of His acceptance. Those who serve God with a sad face because what they are doing is unpleasant are not serving Him. They are bringing a form of homage, but life is absent.

God does not require slaves to grace His throne. He is Lord of the empire of love and His servants dress in robes of joy. The angels of God serve with songs, not with groans. Just a murmur or a sigh would be mutiny because obedience that is not voluntary is disobedience. The Lord looks at the heart, and if we were forced to serve, He would reject our offering. Service coupled with joy is heart service, and heart service is true service.

"The joy of the LORD is your strength" (Nehemiah 8:10). Joy removes difficulties. Joy is to our service as oil is to the wheels of a railroad car. Without oil the axle grows hot and accidents occur. If there is no holy joy to oil our wheels, our spirit will soon be clogged with weariness.

Let me ask you a question. Do you serve the Lord with joy? Then show the people of the world, who think our religion is slavery, that serving God is a delight and a joy.

—CHARLES H. SPURGEON

GOD'S WORDS FOR YOU, GRANDMA

Have the same mindset as Christ Jesus: Who, being in very nature God, did not consider equality with God something to be used to his own advantage; rather, he made himself nothing by taking the very nature of a servant, being made in human likeness.
And being found in appearance as a man, he humbled himself by becoming obedient to death—even death on a cross!

PHILIPPIANS 2:5–8

Serve one another humbly in love.

GALATIANS 5:13

Serve wholeheartedly, as if you were serving the Lord, not people, because you know that the Lord will reward each one for whatever good they do.

EPHESIANS 6:7–8

We have different gifts, according to the grace given to each of us. If your gift is prophesying, then prophesy in accordance with your faith; if it is serving, then serve; if it is teaching, then teach.

ROMANS 12:6–7

Though I am free and belong to no one, I have made myself a slave to everyone, to win as many as possible. . . . I have become all things to all people so that by all possible means I might save some.

1 CORINTHIANS 9:19, 22

“Now that I, your Lord and Teacher, have washed your feet, you also should wash one another’s feet. I have set you an example that you should do as I have done for you.”

JOHN 13:14–15

“Whoever welcomes this little child in my name welcomes me; and whoever welcomes me welcomes the one who sent me. For it is the one who is least among you all who is the greatest.”

LUKE 9:48

Let us then approach God’s throne of grace with confidence, so that we may receive mercy and find grace to help us in our time of need.

HEBREWS 4:16

The LORD has heard my cry for mercy; the LORD accepts my prayer.

PSALM 6:9

We continually ask God . . . that you may live a life worthy of the Lord and please him in every way: bearing fruit in every good work, growing in the knowledge of God, being strengthened with all power according to his glorious might so that you may have great endurance and patience.

COLOSSIANS 1:9–11

40

THE LORD REJOICES

Strength is an inside secret. It comes from the Lord's Spirit in the well of our inner being. Because His strength is limitless, our wells need never be empty. His strength is constantly surging up to give us exactly what we need in every moment.

Zephaniah gives the secret of lasting strength. Note the glorious progression in Zephaniah 3:17: "The LORD your God is with you, the Mighty Warrior who saves. He will take great delight in you; in his love he will no longer rebuke you, but will rejoice over you with singing." First, the Lord takes great delight in you. In spite of all our failures, He has chosen to be our God and to cherish us. Think of it! This gives us the confidence of strength. We belong to God—He's redeemed us in Christ and placed His Spirit in us. He'll never give up on us.

Next, the Lord quiets us with His love. The unqualified, indefatigable love of the Lord gives us confidence, security, and peace. There's no need to prove ourselves or blow our own horns. We can live with calm, winsome joy. And knowing that the Lord rejoices over us frees us to rejoice in Him.

—LLOYD JOHN OGILVIE

GOD'S WORDS FOR YOU, GRANDMA

The Lord gives strength to his people; the Lord blesses his people with peace.

PSALM 29:11

"I will strengthen them in the Lord and in his name they will live securely," declares the Lord.

ZECHARIAH 10:12

He said to me, "My grace is sufficient for you, for my power is made perfect in weakness." Therefore I will boast all the more gladly about my weaknesses, so that Christ's power may rest on me. That is why, for Christ's sake, I delight in weaknesses, in insults, in hardships, in persecutions, in difficulties. For when I am weak, then I am strong.

2 CORINTHIANS 12:9–10

The Lord is the strength of his people, a fortress of salvation for his anointed one.

PSALM 28:8

"In the Lord alone are deliverance and strength."

ISAIAH 45:24

He gives strength to the weary and increases the power of the weak. Even youths grow tired and weary, and young men stumble and fall; but those who hope in the Lord will renew their strength. They will soar on wings like eagles; they will run and not grow weary, they will walk and not be faint.

ISAIAH 40:29-31

Strengthen me according to your word.

PSALM 119:28

Wealth and honor come from you; you are the ruler of all things. In your hands are strength and power to exalt and give strength to all.

1 CHRONICLES 29:12

I pray that out of his glorious riches he may strengthen you with power through his Spirit in your inner being.

EPHESIANS 3:16

I can do all this through him who gives me strength.

PHILIPPIANS 4:13

The eyes of the Lord are on the righteous and his ears are attentive to their prayer, but the face of the Lord is against those who do evil.

1 PETER 3:12

BIBLIOGRAPHY

All excerpts used by permission. Italics in Scripture indicate the author's emphasis.

Arthur, Kay. *Beloved: From God's Heart to Yours*; A Daily Devotional. Harvest House, 1994.

Eppinga, Jacob D. *As Long As I Live: Thoughts on Growing Older.* Faith Alive Christian Resources, 1993.

Gilhuis, Cornelis. *Conversations on Growing Older.* William B. Eerdmans, 1977.

God Is Faithful: MyDaily® Devotional. Thomas Nelson, 2014.

Graham, Billy. *Where I Am: Heaven, Eternity, and Our Life Beyond.* Thomas Nelson, 2015.

Graham, Billy. *Wisdom for Each Day.* Thomas Nelson, 2008.

Jeremiah, Dr. David. *Ever Faithful: A 365-Day Devotional.* Thomas Nelson, 2018.

Jeremiah, Dr. David. *David Jeremiah Morning and Evening Devotions: Holy Moments in the Presence of God.* Thomas Nelson, 2017.

Lucado, Max. *Before Amen: The Power of a Simple Prayer.* Thomas Nelson, 2014.

Lucado, Max. *A Gentle Thunder.* Word, 1995.

Lucado, Max. *On the Anvil: Stories on Being Shaped into God's Image.* Thomas Nelson, 1994.

MacArthur, John. *Drawing Near: Daily Readings for a Deeper Faith.* Crossway Books, 1993.

Manning, Brennan. *Abba's Child: The Cry of the Heart for Intimate Belonging.* NavPress, 1994.

Maxwell, John C. and Jim Dornan. *Becoming a Person of Influence: How to Positively Influence the Lives of Others.* Thomas Nelson, 1997.

Mom's Devotional Bible. With devotions by Elisa Morgan. Zondervan, 1996.

Morgan, Robert J. *Always Near: 10 Ways to Delight in the Closeness of God.* Thomas Nelson, 2019.

Nouwen, Henri J. M. *Our Greatest Gift: A Meditation on Dying and Caring.* HarperCollins, 1994.

Ogilvie, Lloyd John. *Silent Strength for My Life: God's Wisdom for Daily Living.* Harvest House, 1990.

Sanders, J. Oswald. *Enjoying Your Best Years: Staying Young While Growing Older.* Discovery House, 1993.

Schuller, Robert H. *A Walk of Faith: Living Positively One Day at a Time.* Robert Schuller Ministries, 1985.

Shaw, Jean. *The Better Half of Life: Meditations from Ecclesiastes.* Zondervan, 1983.

Smith, Hannah Whitall. *The Christian's Secret of a Happy Life.* 1875.

Stafford, Tim. *As Our Years Increase: Answers to Questions about Retirement, Finances, Health, Changing Relationships, Death*. InterVarsity Press, 1992.

Stoop, Jan and Betty Southard. *The Grandmother Book: Sharing Your Special Joys and Gifts with a New Generation*. Thomas Nelson, 1993.

Swindoll, Charles R. *Laugh Again*. Thomas Nelson, 1992.

Tada, Joni Eareckson. *Diamonds in the Dust: 366 Sparkling Devotions*. Zondervan, 1993.

The Devotional Bible for Dads. With notes by Robert Wolgemuth. Zondervan, 1999.

FAVORITE MEMORIES

FAVORITE MEMORIES

FAVORITE MEMORIES

FAVORITE MEMORIES